Dearest

Mom [illegible]

anoint these words

to your heart!

THE SOVEREIGN GRACE OF GOD

AS SEEN IN

THE LIFE OF JOB

Finally,

BY

GLENNA SALSBURY

Glenna!

SovereignGrace Publishing

Scottsdale, Arizona 85253

2003

THE SOVEREIGN GRACE OF GOD AS SEEN IN THE
LIFE OF JOB

Published by SovereignGrace Publishing

Scottsdale, Arizona   85253

Printed in the United States of America

ISBN 1-59196-358-3

Note: All scriptural quotations are from the King James
Version of the Bible unless otherwise indicated.

DEDICATION

The Apostle Paul, under the influence of the Spirit of God, set forth life-changing truth found in the Book of Romans. All of these doctrinal realities, about the sovereign grace of God, serve as the written Word available to all through the centuries.

The incredible patriarch Job, lived out these truths. His is the "visual art" that shows us God alone is sovereign over all. Job *demonstrated* God's character at work. We *understand* His character through the pen of Paul.

These two saints are two of God's greatest gifts to me. In them and through them He continues to reveal His mercy and His grace. I am eternally grateful to Him and to them.

CONTENTS

FOREWORD

The deep desire of every believer is for growth, for spiritual maturity and so each one of us embarks upon a search to obtain this maturity. The Book of Job reveals the fact that we can trust God Himself to produce that maturity in us! The same simple trust which we exercised when the Holy Spirit revealed to us the work of Christ on the Cross is that with which we can live our life on a daily basis.

Contrary to much of our present dogma, trusting Christ does not involve trying to guess God's will for our life every minute of every day. Neither is it a works program of praying faithfully in order to gain God's favor; nor does it depend upon studying so many hours per week, or reading the right books, or following the right speaker, or confessing our sins often enough, or any other form of performance. God is living His life and plan through us. He, the Life, is causing us to grow. He is in charge of the timing and circumstances of our growth. Because He is God we can trust Him to accomplish His purposes. That is precisely what Job discovered.

If the thought of such freedom in trusting God causes some turmoil in your mind, recall the words of Paul. *"For we can do nothing against the truth, but for the truth."* (II Corinthians 13:8) The God of the Universe will protect and preserve the Truth of His Word. It was with this same assurance that the teacher Gamaliel stated, *"If this counsel or this work be of men, it will come to nothing, but if it be of God, ye cannot overthrow it, lest perhaps ye be found even to fight against God."* (Acts 5:38,39)

With these words of assurance I submit to you the reading of this book. May the words of my pen and the meditation of the reader's heart be acceptable in Thy sight, O Lord. Together we thank You for the Holy Spirit Who will guide us into all Truth. (John 16:13)

vii

PREFACE

Most scholars believe that the Book of Job is the oldest book in the Bible. Job appears to have lived at about the time of Abraham, also known as the period of the Patriarchs. E.W. Bullinger (1837-1913), an ardent Biblical scholar and direct descendent of the great Swiss reformer, Johann H. Bullinger, has written in his commentary on Job: *"The Book of Job carries us back to the remote past, and contains the oldest lesson in the world. It is significant that this oldest book should be devoted to imparting that knowledge, in comparison with which all other knowledge sinks into insignificance. It is the lesson which is essential to our having peace with God for Time and to our enjoying the peace of God for Eternity."* 1

Think of it! The amazing knowledge in the Book of Job is that "with which all other knowledge sinks into insignificance!" It is the lesson that provides "peace with God" here and in eternity!

Bullinger goes on to provide marvelous commentary on the significant reference to Job in the Book of James: *"Ye have heard of the patience of Job and have seen the end of the Lord; that the Lord is very pitiful, and of tender mercy."* (James 5:11)

Most believers have heard a great deal about "the patience of Job" and have even fallen into the works-oriented trap of trying to emulate Job's patience. Yet the key question is not if you have heard about the patience of Job, but rather have you seen "the end of the Lord." The Book of Job is about revelation (seeing). It is about *"knowing God"* (Philippians 3:10) in His true character rather than through humanistic, philosophical insights.

The *"end of the Lord"* is His work in expanding our knowledge to see that God alone is the possessor of righteousness. There is no good thing in us (Romans 3: 10,11) and God alone is the *"bestower of His own righteousness."* 2   He demonstrates this through His tender mercy extended in saving grace to those whom He calls.

On the other hand, man is always attempting to be religious to create a righteousness that can be gained or improved on through man's good efforts. No! The *"end of the Lord"* is to bring us thoroughly to the end of ourselves, even to the end of our own understanding of Him. Amen!

"I have heard of thee by the hearing of the ear, but now mine eye seeth thee. Wherefore I abhor myself and repent in dust and ashes." (Job 42:5, 6). Here is the response of one who has truly seen God in His sovereignty and His righteousness.

Bullinger goes on to catalog other Biblical illustrations of saints in whose lives the Lord chose to give this revelation. They include:

  * The Prodigal Son's revelation. *"And the son said unto him, Father, I have sinned against heaven, and in thy sight, and am no more worthy to be called thy son."* Luke 15:21)

  * The Famine's work in Joseph's brothers. *"We are verily guilty."* (Genesis 44:16)

  * Nathan's Parable for David. *"I have sinned against the Lord."* (2 Samuel 12:1-13)

  * Isaiah's Vision. *"I am undone...unclean."* (Isaiah 6:1-5)

  * Daniel's Vision. *"Therefore I was left alone, and saw the great vision, and there remained no strength in me: for my comeliness was turned in me into corruption, and I retained no strength."* 3

In each of these lives, including that of Job, circumstances were brought to bear upon a believer who in turn had to fall upon his face before the Lord and experience by revelation his own condemnation and helplessness outside of the work of a sovereign Lord who is *"very pitiful and of tender mercy!"* This is the lesson God is teaching us through His hand on the life of Job.

It is also significant that Job is one of the longest books in the Bible. This may well indicate the added weight the Lord gives to the importance of the message contained within its pages.

Just think about this staggering reality. The Book of Job consists of forty-two chapters of the Bible devoted to one single believer's life. Certainly this fact alone serves as a signal from the Lord Himself that this message is a very important one from God's perspective!

It would be very helpful to have your Bible open to the Book of Job as you read this commentary. This will allow you to saturate your mind with God's word as you consider these insights.

Another helpful action would be to turn to the *Closing Thoughts* section at the back of the book. There you will find eight truths in the Book of Job, which may be especially meaningful to you as you study. Ask the Lord to speak to you as you consider these realities.

May His Spirit apply His revelation to your heart and life as you read these words for God's glory and for your personal encouragement and understanding.

CHAPTER ONE

THE SAGA OF SUFFERING

A young man came to me not long ago out of sheer desperation. He related, "I have been a Christian for a year and a half now. There's nothing I want more than to really live for Jesus Christ. But, honestly, I'm just going downhill. In fact, you may not believe this, but I actually think I'm losing my mind."

As we talked, Bill shared with me the mental torture, which he had been experiencing. He told of having terrific fears of Satan and satanic pressures. He experienced horrifying nightmares; he found himself continually thinking about the supernatural world, sensing pure fear and terror even at his own thought patterns. During the months of this torment he had been looking within himself for the answers to what was causing this phenomenon. He asked me, "What is it that I am failing to do as a Christian? I have prayed again and again for relief. I've asked the Lord to show me what sin is in my life. Where is the joy and peace which is supposed to be in my life?"

Now I would like to ask you what you would have said to my friend. Think about your answer for a moment. Perhaps you would have suggested he seek psychological counseling. Maybe you would have recommended a good book that has recently been meaningful to you in your own Christian experience.

Another suggestion might have been increased prayer. All of these, plus several other alternatives, are certainly possibilities as a means of obtaining temporary help. Yet there is a deeper understanding that God desires for us to have about His ways in our life. Every situation that a believer faces, good or bad, is ultimately from the hand of the Father Who has a high purpose in mind for His children. Growth is His purpose.

It is this system for growth that is visible in the saga of Job. As a believer begins to understand something of the higher purposes of God in his or her life, he will suddenly find himself trusting the One who is in charge of the growth process. My friend Bill discovered this freedom and understanding even in the midst of his mental trials as the Holy Spirit taught him from Job's life.

In the world of nature growth cannot begin until the seed is planted. So it is in the world of the spirit. We cannot grow in our Christian life until we have received the Seed planted within. Peter writes, *"Being born again, not of corruptible seed, but of incorruptible, by the word of God, which liveth and abideth forever."* (I Peter 1:23) It is God himself who plants the Life within us prior to which we cannot begin to grow. And so we read, *"Blessed be the God and Father of our Lord Jesus Christ, Who, according to His abundant mercy, hath begotten us again unto a living hope by the resurrection of Jesus Chris t from the dead."* (I Peter 1:3) James writes, *"Of His own will begat He us with the Word of Truth, that we should be a kind of first fruits of His creatures."* (James 1:18) John confirms that *"As many as received Him (Jesus Christ), to them gave He power to become the children of God even to them that believe on His name; who were born, not of blood, nor of the will of the flesh, nor of the will of man, but of God."* (John 1:12,13)

There is no life until we have received the Life, Jesus Christ, which occurs as God grants us the grace to come to Him for salvation and plants His life within us in the person of the Holy Spirit. He is the one who baptizes with the Spirit and from whom we receive Life, abundant and eternal.

Now begins the growth process. Each believer begins to hunger after a deeper relationship with the Lord Who has come to live within. Individually we begin to search for ways to enhance our Christian experience.

The search may vary to some degree in each life, but generally it begins with the reading of good books written about the Christian life. These often include *The Christian's Secret for a Happy Life; The Greatest Thing in the World; Victorious Christian Living; Prayer, Conversing with God;* etc.

As we read these books we gain bits of insight, but as time passes we drop into the feelings of failure and inadequacy once again. So, we often attempt to increase our prayer effort and perhaps even succeed at disciplining ourselves into longer periods of prayer but the time comes when questions begin. "Does God really care about me? Why is He not answering my requests? Am I not praying correctly? I must not have enough faith. The sinful habits and weaknesses which I see in my life must be preventing God from answering."

So our pace quickens and intensifies. Usually it takes us to an increasing number of Christian meetings, speakers, conferences and activities. Again we have needs met for the moment. We often escape the feelings of emptiness with momentary accomplishments in Christian service, or we become elated over some new insight into the Truth. The pattern continues, nevertheless. We wake up one day feeling empty and dry again.

Our next effort may be in the direction of increased Bible study. We determine to spend more time in the Word. The results may prove encouraging for a while in that we do feel better for having known in our own heart that this morning we spent thirty minutes in the Word. But often it happens that the more we read, the greater condemnation we experience. We read passages that exhort us to *"Flee youthful lusts."* (II Timothy 2:22), *"Abstain from all appearance of evil."* (I Thessalonians 5:22), *"Whatever ye do, do all to the glory of God."* (I Corinthians 10:31), *"Pray without ceasing."* (I Thessalonians 5:17)

As we compare our life against the Word we increasingly see how far short we fall from God's desires for us. The result is often varying degrees of depression and discouragement. As we read these exhortations unto holiness we cry out with Paul, *"Oh, wretched man that I am, who shall deliver me from the body of this death?"* And the answer comes, *"I thank God through Jesus Christ, our Lord."* (Romans 7:24,25).

Personally, I can recall the early years of my Christian walk in which I read all the books and agonized over my own sin and failure as a believer. My heart and my actions were often a disgrace to the kingdom of God. My desire was to be obedient, yet I seemed powerless to live in obedience.

One Sunday morning remains particularly vivid in my mind. I was the mother of two little girls, married to a godly man, and we were in full-time Christian ministry. My husband and I were seated in church and the pastor was preaching from John 7:37 and 38.

"In the last day, that great day of the feast, Jesus stood and cried out saying, If any man thirst, let him come unto me and drink. He that believeth on me, as the scripture hath said, out of his heart shall flow rivers of living water."

As I listened my heart cried out in utter desperation. I told the Lord that my life did not even have a trickle flowing, let alone a river! I longed for His life to flow from me to others, and I begged him to reveal to me what was missing in my life.

Soon after that the Holy Spirit began to teach me life-changing truths from the Book of Romans. I began to see that every aspect of what unfolds in my life, from salvation, through His sanctifying work, to my entrance into glory is His work and flows directly from His hand. Then, in His grace, He led me to see these truths as displayed in the life of Job.

My life has never been the same. Rivers of living water, and the joy and freedom of walking in the Savior, have continued to unfold, even in the darkest situations, because of the revelation of grace and mercy from the Word by His Spirit. This is the great message that He brings to us through Job's life.

God's ways are exceedingly simple and uncomplicated *"For the preaching of the cross is to them that perish foolishness; but unto us who are saved it is the power of God."* (I Corinthians 1:18) To the finite mind it truly is foolishness to think that by simply believing that Jesus Christ died for our sinfulness – our humanness and by looking to Him for forgiveness, we have received total cleansing and have been stamped as righteous as God Himself. (II Corinthians 5:21) Yet God has declared it so.

This same simplicity is the basis for understanding the growth process. And the growth process is God's plan for deliverance, uniquely tailored to fit the needs of each of our lives! God says, *"As ye have, therefore, received Christ Jesus the Lord, so walk ye in Him."* (Colossians 2:6) How did we receive Him? What did we do? Absolutely nothing! Oh, but we say, "I claimed His Word as Truth. I chose to receive Him. I repented of my sin. I obeyed His will."

Isn't it strange how many "I's" there are in the statements above? Let's review what God says our part is in believing: *"of His own will begot he us," "who according to His abundant mercy, hath begotten us," "who were born, not of blood, nor of the will of the flesh, nor or the will of man, but of God."* (John 1:13)

In addition, we read *"No man can come to me, except the Father who hath sent me draw him."* (John 6:44), *"Ye have not chosen me, but I have chosen you and ordained you"* (John 15:16), and *"Who hath resisted his will?"* (Romans 9:19)

Finally, we read, *"The god of this age hath blinded the minds of them who believe not* (that included you and me in days past) *lest the light of the glorious gospel of Christ, who is the image of God, should shine unto them.*" (II Corinthians 4:4) But now God "*has commanded the light to shine out of darkness, and hath shone in our hearts to give the light of the knowledge of the glory of God in the face of Jesus Christ.*" (II Corinthians 4:6)

The Scripture clearly states that we were blind to Christ until God enlightened us, and it was then that we were "*delivered from the power of darkness, and translated into the kingdom of his dear Son.*" (Colossians 1:13)

And so we must conclude that salvation is all of grace, God's grace. Therefore, the Christian walk will also be by grace, totally, God's grace.

"*As ye have therefore received Christ Jesus the Lord, so walk ye in Him.*" (Colossians 2:6)

He revealed Himself to those He chose before the world began (Ephesians 1:4); He drew us to Himself and now He is living His life through us. His ultimate purpose is to conform us to the image of Jesus Christ. (Romans 8:29) That is exactly why Romans 8:28 precedes Romans 8:29: "*All things*" are working together for good to accomplish His purpose in our lives, as conformity to the image of His Son!

And so we have the privilege, and sometimes the pain, of watching Him work this plan into our life. "*For it is God who worketh in you both to will and to do of His good pleasure.*" (Philippians 2:13) He will work in His own sovereign way and time. He alone is the Deliverer who frees us from our ongoing struggle with our fleshly weaknesses, again and again, for as long as we walk on earth in these bodies!

Because we know His character we can trust His means for accomplishing His plan in us. We will not determine how and when He works anymore than we determined His revelation of Himself in salvation. *"And He doeth according to His will in the army of heaven, and among the inhabitants of the earth, and none can stay his hand, or say unto Him, What doest thou?"* (Daniel 4:35b)

 "*For unto you is given in the behalf of Christ, not only to believe on Him, but also to suffer for His sake.*" (Philippians 1:29) Have you ever seen that truth before? If so, did you find that you read over it with the conscious or unconscious idea that somehow Paul was writing to first century Christians or a special group of Christians and that it certainly did not apply to you? Or perhaps you thought to yourself, "Well, I'm certainly thankful that I have never had to suffer like some people I know." Then your mind trails off to martyrs, or to those who have had unusual pain or tragedy. The fact is, more often than not, we simply fail to recognize the hand of God in our lives in the area of suffering.

For example, can you imagine what Peter must have suffered within himself after having denied the Lord Jesus? Yet the very denial was ordained in Peter's life by the Lord Himself. Peter wanted to be faithful to the Lord. He even spoke his allegiance, "*Though all men shall be offended because of Thee, yet will I never be offended.*" (Matthew 26:33b) Then repeats his commitment and his "willingness" in verse 35. Jesus had another plan for Peter. "*And the Lord said, Simon, Simon, behold Satan hath desired to have you, that he may sift you as wheat. But I have prayed for thee, that thy faith fail not*" (Luke 22:31, 32b)

Satan, as was also true in the life of Job, had to request permission from the Lord to have power over Peter's actions. And when the Lord gave permission to Satan He also set boundaries upon Satan's power. Yet Peter's personal desire and will had been to be obedient and faithful. "*Lord, I am ready to go with thee, both into prison, and to death.*" (Luke 22:33) And Peter suffered in his

21

failure and sin. *"And Peter went out, and wept bitterly."* (Luke 22:62)

Peter discovered his own inability to live the Christian life. This was an essential lesson. It was through this satanic attack that Peter learned of his own helplessness. He learned to rely on the Lord's strength for deliverance, even from the Evil One.

The Apostle Paul's sufferings came in a variety of circumstances and problems. Yet the most persistent and troublesome suffering came from Satan himself, even though mighty Paul prayed for Satan's power to be withdrawn! *"And lest I should be exalted above measure through the abundance of the revelations there was given to me a thorn in the flesh, the messenger of Satan to buffet me. For this thing I besought the Lord thrice, that it might depart from me. And he said unto me, my grace is sufficient for thee; for my strength is made perfect in weakness."* (II Corinthians 12:7-9b)

Here are two graphic examples of believers who were ordained by the Lord Himself to experience suffering. It is *"given"* to us for a purpose in the same sovereign way believing was given to us. (Reread Philippians 1:29) When we experience trials, tribulations and sufferings, we quickly see the weakness of our flesh. It is only then that we begin to truly seek to be comforted by the Creator and to learn to trust His sovereign ways in our life. This is the essence of our faith.

It is in the life of Job that we most clearly see the infinite details of suffering as the means by which God produces His character in us. This suffering also reveals to us the sovereignty of God, His very character. As we proceed, we will get a glimpse into what God is doing in us as we see

Him work in Job. Why? Because the principle remains the same for every believer, "*not only to believe but also to suffer.*" And this suffering is designed by Him for our highest good, that we might learn to walk with utter reliance on the Father's faithful work in our lives.

CHAPTER TWO

JOB, THE PERFECT MAN

"There was a man in the land of Uz, whose name was Job; and that man was perfect and upright, and one that feared God, and shunned evil." Job 1:1

The Bible states that Job was a perfect man. Have you ever met a perfect human being? Neither have I. Was Job a human? Yes. Then what does the Bible mean when it says he was perfect? It certainly does not mean that God judged Job perfect because he did so many good things or because he tried so hard to please God. As we read in Isaiah 64:6, *"all our righteousnesses are as filthy rags"* in God's sight. No human being, therefore, will ever be good enough, by God's standard of measurement, through any amount of self-effort.

Where, then, did Job get his "righteousness?" What did he do to be counted as perfect in the eyes of God? According to Hebrews 11:7 the men and women in the Old Testament who obtained a right standing with God (righteousness) received their perfection through faith, through simply believing God, as He revealed Himself to them. (Romans 4:3) We see this faith in Job immediately as he begins to suffer. *"The Lord gave and the Lord hath taken away; blessed be the name of the Lord,"* (Job 1:21b) As his suffering intensified and Job felt he might die, we still hear his confession of faith. *"For I know that my Redeemer liveth and that he shall stand at the latter day upon the earth...in my flesh shall I see God."* (Job 19:25, 26b) Job believed in his own bodily resurrection and in the Lord's millennial reign on earth, by faith! This is the reason Job is called "perfect." He believed in the Messiah by faith.

This is also true today. *"Faith comes by hearing and hearing by the word of God."* (Romans 10:17) As we believe God's Word, through the revelation of the Holy Spirit, we receive the righteousness of God Himself. Therefore, we, like Job, can be called "perfect."

"And there were born unto him seven sons and three daughters. His substance also was seven thousand sheep, and three thousand camels, and five hundred yoke of oxen, and five hundred she-asses, and a very great household; so that this man was the greatest of all the men of the east. And his sons went and feasted in their houses, every one his day, and sent and called for their three sisters to eat and to drink with them. And it was, when the days of their feasting were finished that Job sent and sanctified them, and rose up early in the morning, and offered burnt offerings according to the number of them all; for Job said, It may be that my sons have sinned, and cursed God in their hearts. Thus did Job continually." (Job 1:2-5)

Job is the picture of a committed, respected believer. Apparently he was a fine father; he prayed regularly for his children. He is described as the *"greatest of all the men of the east."* This includes not only his great wealth, but also his position of esteem among his countrymen. He was consistent in his life of worship and devotion to the Lord, as the Scripture says he prayed *"continually."*

Things seem pretty terrific in Job's life, don't they? In our current vernacular we would say he seemed to have his life together. He was living the "balanced life." He was healthy, wealthy and wise...a great businessman, a good father, the spiritual head of his home.

Many of us as believers can relate to some of this "ideal" world of Job. We may have come to know Christ and experienced a fair amount of "normalcy" and happiness. Then some strange events may have begun to occur...things that unsettled our "ideal" world.

There is a pattern to God's work in the life of His own. When the Holy Spirit comes to dwell in the life of a believer, He gives each of us a new heart, a new mind and new desires. From this new heart begins to spring a desire to be totally committed to, completely involved with, this One who has come to live in us. We may begin to pray with Paul, *"That I may know Him, and the power of His resurrection, and the fellowship of his sufferings, being made conformable unto his death."* (Philippians 3:10) Or we may have simply prayed to know Him better or find His will, or be a "better Christian."

Soon God begins to fulfill these longings in us through a personal breaking process that usually consists of being held in an "uncomfortable" position somewhere in our lives. We did not expect this kind of an answer! It is through this process that the Lord is bringing our outward actions more and more in line with that inward righteousness and perfection through which God views us. Like Job, we find ourselves crying out in confusion and pain.

The Pain of Personal Experience

Not many years after my own experience of seeing the sovereign grace of God begin to unfold in my understanding, I found myself in one of those "breaking" experiences. I became blinded by the desires of my own flesh and buffeted by the attack of the Evil One. The end result was a difficult divorce, much condemnation by many in my Christian world of friends and colleagues, plus my own inner agony over my failure as a believer.

Thus began an entirely new work of God in my life, showing Himself faithful in my faithlessness and teaching me some of the life-giving truths of being set free by the truth of His righteousness. Job's story continues to impact my understanding of the Lord's hand in my daily walk.

In Job 1:6-12 we discover that God has a plan for Job's life. Needless to say, it was not anything that Job had in mind! *"Now there was a day when the sons of God came to present themselves before the Lord, and Satan came also among them. And the Lord said unto Satan, Whence comest thou? Then Satan answered the Lord, and said, From going to and fro in the earth, and from walking up and down in it. And the Lord said unto Satan, Hast thou considered my servant, Job, that there is none like him in the earth, a perfect and an upright man, one who feareth God, and shunneth evil? Then Satan answered the Lord, and said, Doth Job fear God for nothing? Hast not thou made an hedge about him, and about his house, and about all that he hath on every side? Thou hast blessed the work of his hands, and his substance is increased in the land. But put forth thine hand now, and touch all that he hath, and he will curse thee to thy face. And the Lord said unto Satan, behold, all that he hath is in thy power; only upon himself put not forth thine hand. So Satan went forth from the presence of the Lord."* Job 1:6-12

There are some interesting things to note about this conversation. First, Satan has access to heaven. Even in the New Testament he is still spoken of as the accuser of the brethren. Secondly, note that it was the Lord Himself who drew Satan's attention to Job. Yet we know the Lord described Job as *"perfect, upright, fearing God and shunning evil."*

In other words, God Himself has stated that the happenings that are about to overtake Job are not in any way a result of something evil in Job. Job was not guilty of some hidden sin, (not even the subtle sin of pride, which some critics have attributed to him). He had perfect standing in God's eyes.

Next, it is interesting to see that God is the One who gives Satan permission to touch the lives of saints. And, He sets boundaries on Satan's activities. Satan is the source of evil, but God is sovereign over all evil and consciously uses evil to accomplish His own purpose. (Isaiah 45:7:Amos 3:6)

Finally, we need to see that a record of this heavenly conversation must have been given to the author of Job at some later date through a vision, a dream or direct revelation. If we can believe the miracle of the resurrection, we can accept the possibility of God working in this way for the purpose of teaching us about Himself.

Satan's logic is simple. He states that Job worships and serves God simply because the Lord has been so good to Job. But, Satan suggests, if God mistreats Job a little he will curse God.

Verse twelve gives God's unique answer to Satan. *"And the Lord said unto Satan, "Behold, all that he hath is in thy power; only upon himself put not forth thine hand."* It was God who gave Satan the privileges with Job. It was also God who set the limits upon how far Satan could go with Job.

Did Job select this plan for his life? Did Job, by his actions, deserve the calamities that were about to descend upon him? Did Job have any way of knowing about the heavenly conversation at this point in his life? Did Job know that it was his own beloved Lord who had ordained that which was about to come upon him? The answer, of course, in each case is negative.

In Job 1:13-19 we read the carefully outlined details of the calamities that strike in Job's life. The hundreds of oxen and asses, which were his, are stolen, and his servants are killed by marauders. Next, lightning burns up his sheep and the shepherds. The enemy steals his three thousand camels and kills the camel keepers. Finally, a tornado-type wind destroys his ten children as they are sharing a family dinner. The house comes down upon their heads.

Put yourself in Job's predicament for a moment, mentally. Imagine those things that might happen in your life that in some way could compare to these calamities. Try now to picture what *your* reaction would be. Here is Job's reaction, *"Naked came I out of my mother's womb, and naked shall I return there. The Lord gave, and the Lord hath taken away; blessed be the name of the Lord"* (Job 1:21)

There is a picture of faith - walking! Isn't it interesting to note that Job saw all that had just happened as from the hand of the Lord? Yet you and I know from the conversation that took place in heaven that these tragedies passed through the hand of Satan enroute to Job.

Some Bible scholars and teachers on platforms today would be horrified at the thought of "blaming" such tragedies upon God. Perhaps they should review the case of Job and the case of Peter and even Christ Himself at the Crucifixion. The Scriptures tell us that it pleased the Father to bruise His own Son. (Isaiah 53:9,10) Surely there is a mystery surrounding what this God of Love does to accomplish His highest purposes!

Job knew enough about the Person of the Lord that at this moment he felt confident in giving thanks, knowing that this was the will of God for his life. Job had come to God by faith initially, believing Him to be trustworthy. Now, as he received his relationship with the Father by faith, he is walking with that faith in action, trusting God's dealings with him to be for his very best. Job also understood enough about the sovereign working of God that at this point in his life he doesn't question even that that seems undeserved and illogical.

Job's childlike trust in the midst of tragedy may overwhelm us. We say, "I could never have that kind of faith." However, the fact of the matter is that, once you and I have received Jesus Christ into our lives, He begins to supply us with the measure of faith we need for the circumstances we will encounter. (Romans 12: 3, 6)

Often we discover in some small crisis that the proportion of our faith is more than we had imagined. That is because God has met our need for an increased supply of faith in a situation that required the increase. (Philippians 4:19) After this has occurred in our lives a few times, we begin to discover by experience that we can trust God. This is what growth is all about. Bit by bit, step by step, our faith increases as He stretches us out upon Himself.

In Job 2:1-8 we again overhear the conversation between God and Satan. Again the Lord is the one who initiates the conversation and reminds Satan of His perfect servant, Job. Satan points out that the only reason Job has not yet cursed God is because Job has not suffered physically. The Lord grants Satan permission now to bring horrible physical suffering upon Job. The only restriction set is that Satan cannot kill Job.

Think of it! The loving, good, kind God of the Universe has ordained horrible physical suffering to befall His own perfect child. The disease itself will come at the hand of Satan; yet the One who has given permission and set the limits of the suffering is God Himself. This is the reason Paul could, with great confidence, pen the words of II Thessalonians 3:3, *"But the Lord is faithful, who shall establish you and keep you from evil."*

Obviously the Father keeps his servants from every form of satanic attack, which He has not ordained for them. Thus, all that befalls the believer is that which eventually *"works together for good"* and, therefore, ultimately can be seen as good from God's perspective, as He knows the end from the beginning. For this reason, Jesus taught us to pray, *"Lead us not into temptation, but deliver us from evil."* (Matthew 6:13). Literally, the verse reads *"deliver us from the evil one!"*

Think of how the truth of God's sovereignty in this area frees us to worship Him and trust Him. We can become preoccupied with Him and Him alone, not concentrating on self or Satan. Only then is it possible to *"Trust in the Lord with all thine heart and lean not unto thine own understanding."* (Proverbs 3:5)

Yet is it not true that today our traditional dogma has sorely complicated such a life of simple trust? We are told, *"Trust in the Lord with all thine heart and lean not unto thine own understanding,"* and "Be certain that you are truly yielded, completely prayed up, free from any known sin, spending time in the Word, watching out for Satan's hand in your circumstances, and listening to the voice of God!" Then, we are told, if all of the above are true, *"He shall direct thy paths."* (Proverbs 3:6b)

When we finish our checklist on all the requirements for effective trusting, we discover that God certainly cannot be trusted to work in our life because we are such failures in one or more of the areas which are requirements for making that verse work! One wants to ask, "How yielded is yielded enough? By whose standards are we measuring? Does yieldedness come through the performance of certain duties?"

On the contrary, none of these "requirements" appear in God's Word when He outlines trusting. He simply states that He is trustworthy; therefore, we can trust Him in every detail that enters our life. He has already judged us perfect because we have become His children by faith in His Son. (II Corinthians 5:21)

Perhaps one of the greatest heresies in the church today resides in the false teaching surrounding man's ability to control the hand of God through works, self-effort or other actions and attitudes. The end result of this teaching that emphasizes man's power and ability is a preoccupation with self. Believers are caught in the terrible trap of constant self-examination. This results in self-condemnation, guilt and depression or in pride, an outsized ego, and a judgmental attitude toward others.

Returning to the predicament of Job, we discover the pressures in his crisis are now increasing. He finds himself in extreme physical pain, covered with huge running boils over every inch of his body, ears, mouth, feet, hair, etc.

In addition, Satan was no fool; he knew he had an ally in Job's wife. He had been certain that she was left intact. It is she who adds to Job's temptations and trials. She says, "Don't tell me you are still going to trust God when He is doing this to you. Curse Him and die." (Job 2:9 loosely translated) Now there is real comfort!

Almost all of us can identify in some way with this scene. Somewhere in our own Christian experience, when things have not been going too well, there has been someone, a spouse or relative or friend, who said, "So this is what being a Christian does for you!" Even we ourselves often become burdened with a preoccupation with our own failure or circumstances, instead of calling on the Lord in utter dependence and trust.

Job's response is so very basic and childlike. "*Shall we receive good at the hand of God, and shall we not receive evil?*" (Job 2:10) How many of us, steeped in dogma, would answer, "Perish the thought!" God is not the author of evil." And we might smugly quote verses like James 1:13, "*Let no man say when he is tempted, I am tempted of God; for God cannot be tempted with evil, neither tempteth he any man.*"

Our thinking is so finite. Of course, God is not the *source* of evil. If He were, He could not be totally good; yet nothing happens outside of God's specific control. If it did, God would not be sovereign. Job certainly knew that he himself could not control the events that had come into his life. Therefore, he realized that God Himself was in control.

Because he was a child of God, he expected God's very best to be operating in his behalf: even through that which outwardly appeared to be evil.

If the Book of Job ended at this point, some of us would have a tremendous opportunity to receive exhortation. Several sermons could be preached on the faithfulness of Job. The exhortation would follow that we should each one trust God in our circumstances, just as Job did. And we would be tremendously inspired by a sermon like that. The Holy Spirit would use His Word to energize within us a life of trust - until we failed somewhere along the line. At the point of our failure we can be so very grateful that God chose to tell the rest of Job's story.

Before considering the next events in the life of Job it would be good to review the facts that have prepared and qualified Job for the continuing growth process.

First, he was a servant of the Most High God, considered perfect in all his ways because he had placed his faith in the Lord. Secondly, his relationship with God is evidenced by the faith that he demonstrated in spite of overwhelming circumstances.

Now God in His matchless grace is going to bring Job into a deeper understanding of Himself - that Job *"may know Him, and the power of his resurrection, and the fellowship of his sufferings, being made conformable unto his death."* (Philippians 3:10) The process will involve further suffering for Job.

CHAPTER THREE

METHODS OF MATURITY

As we look around in creation, we find that nature teaches us a great deal about the workings of God. When a tree is formed it begins as a seed planted, and the seed has nothing to do with the planting of itself. The Bible speaks of the new birth as analogous to planting a seed. *"Being born again, not of corruptible seed, but of incorruptible, by the word of God, which liveth and abideth forever."* (1 Peter 1:23) Faith came by hearing and hearing came by the word of God; thus, the new life in us is something that the Holy Spirit has planted. This being true, His life principle is that which is going to spring up.

When an oak tree is planted in the form of an acorn, that seed contains in it all that the oak tree will eventually be. Within the seed lies the basic principles for all that will evolve in the growth process of the tree. So, when Christ comes to dwell in a believer, it is His life that will begin to grow within. *"It is the Lord who is faithful; He will establish you."* (II Thessalonians 3:3)

A variety of forces are brought to bear on the life of a tree. They include physical things: the rain, sun, and wind. All are necessary factors in the shaping of a tree. The rain, often coming down in torrents, is just as necessary as the warm sun. The wind makes a great deal of difference to a cypress tree, often creating some fascinating shapes and sizes in these trees. And so with us, the Lord uses some natural forces to bend us and shape us in the direction that He intends for us to grow. In the analogy, He controls the "rain, the sun, and the wind" of our life.

If a tree is planted in the garden, the gardener has much to say about where the tree is placed and how it grows. Sometimes a gardener stakes a tree. He says, essentially, "I want this tree to grow in just this spot and to this allotted height. It will have this specific shape, also."

The tree is literally limited or tied to that spot, and there is no way in which it can cry out, "I don't like this place in the yard. I will take up my roots and move." God is the gardener of our life. He says, "I'm shaping you because I know just how you will fit into the overall plan which I have for my garden."

One of the most beautiful books in the Old Testament confirms this picture of God as the gardener. In the Song of Solomon, we read again and again of this relationship. The Bride is described as a garden. "*A garden enclosed is my sister, my spouse; thy plants are an orchard.*" (Song of Solomon 4:12, 13a) The Bride responds, "*Let my Beloved come to his garden and eat his pleasant fruits.*" (Song of Solomon 4:16) We see that there is a love relationship going on that is intimate and sacred. It is a picture of Christ and His Bride…made up of us as individual believers.

Among trees there are those that produce fruit, those that produce flowers, and those that are simply trees of refreshment - shade trees. Yet each kind and variety of tree has its purpose. Following the analogy, which kind of tree would you prefer to be?

Personally, I would probably select the fruit tree because it could be of practical value. People could come to me in their hunger and I could feed them. But my children, when they were young, were fond of shade trees. They had a shade tree that provided many happy hours for them. It held their tree house!

The God of the Universe has a plan for each of us as believers. We will fulfill different purposes in His plan. We will not all experience the general popularity of the fruit tree, or the leisure and comfort of the shade tree, nor will we all suffer the physical stresses of a cypress tree.

Paraphrasing some verses out of Romans 12, we read: *"God has dealt to every man a particular measure of faith. We are many members in one body, but all of us do not have the same office. Some of us will give forth the Gospel; some will minister to others; some will teach God's Word; some will exhort other believers; some will give money to those in need; some will just smile and give kind words where needed. Included in these ministries will be seen active love, diligent prayer, hospitality and humility."*

God brings the forces into our lives that will equip us to minister in the area of the Body that He planned for us before the foundation of the world (Ephesians 2:10).

Are we rejoicing and actively thanking the Lord for the forces at work in our lives? Are we, each day, praising Him for His faithfulness in conforming us to the image of His

Son in spite of our faithlessness? Or are we sometimes frustrated about our life because it isn't working out the way we had it planned?

A tree does not spring up overnight. The growth process is stage by stage. The life principle within the seed determines how long it will take for a particular tree to mature. Oak trees will take longer than fruit trees. And with the Christian, we will grow according to God's timetable for maturity. He knows what kind of "tree" He has ordained each of us to be.

Seasonal stages are inherent in the growth process of trees. For instance, there is the green shoot stage where everything looks healthy and alive in the tree. Then may come the "nuisance stage"; the leaves begin to fall. There has been growth, but now the tree may be a bit of a bother. The leaves clutter up the yard; the neighbors sometimes fuss about the leaves drifting over into their swimming pool. A degree of irritation toward the tree may come at this stage. The sap runs, or the branches fall off, or something disconcerting often happens in growth.

Of course, we see the parallel. New Christians often show a tremendous spurt of growth at birth, the green shoot stage. They may say things like, "This is so wonderful. I didn't know life could be so great!" But then the 'nuisance stage' may follow. The believer doesn't look so healthy. Other Christians may be quick to point the finger at the problems that this young one is creating.

Winter comes in the life of a tree. The greenery is gone; the leaves have fallen; the nuisance has ended. There is just nothing going on outwardly. The tree appears to be dead! In this stage there is usually no visible fruit, no flowers, and not even any shade available from that tree. One who does not understand trees might say, "That tree is dead; we need to cut it down. There's no hope for that tree." Yet, you and

I know that this stage in the life of a tree is to be expected and it is indispensable for growth.

This same principle applies to believers. God takes us through that which may appear on the outside to be a dead stage, but He is strengthening us inwardly. Eventually the outward manifestations of the inner growth will appear. That is called "fruit!"

In the spring and summer the pruning process begins. If the gardener desires for a tree to bear healthy fruit or flowers he trims it back a bit. God never quits shaping us in this way. In Hebrews 12:6 we read, *every son will be scourged.*" Those whom God loves, His own plants, will be the very ones who are especially selected for the painful pruning process. He is a faithful Gardener!

Finally, the harvest comes. The life principle within the tree produced the fruit or the flower, or the shady leaves that appear. And so the Scripture says, *"As the branch cannot bear fruit of itself, except it abide in the vine, no more can ye, except ye abide in me for without me ye can do nothing."* (John 15:4, 5b) God Himself will produce the fruit in the believer.

Job Experiences Growth

In the first two chapters of Job we saw a picture of harvest time in Job's growth. He was looking very healthy. In the midst of trial he boldly said, *"The Lord gave, and the Lord hath taken away; blessed be the name of the Lord."* (Job 1:21b) But now we will see the winter set in for Job. The leaves are falling. He is going to be an irritation to others and there will be some outward signs of deadness.

In Job 2:11 we read, *"When Job's three friends heard of all this evil that was come upon him, they came everyone from his own place."* The Bible does not indicate that Job invited them to come to him.

Note, please, that what has befallen Job is termed "evil" in the Scripture and these friends have analyzed these events as evil too.

Surmising the attitude in the hearts of Job's friends (based on their conversations which follow), they arrived thinking, "Now isn't this strange. Here was a fine believer. I remember how committed he was. I wonder what he has done, what sin has crept into his life. God certainly would not allow such horrible things to happen to a truly yielded believer."

The men who came were Eliphaz, the Temanite; and Bildad, the Shuhite; and Zophar, the Naamathite. In Job 2:11 we read, *"They had made an appointment together to come to mourn with him and to comfort him."* (Keep in mind their purpose, because we soon discover they do not fulfill their purpose of comforting.)

"When they lifted up their eyes afar off, and knew him not, they lifted up their voice and wept; and they tore everyone his mantle, and sprinkled dust upon their heads toward heaven." These friends realized that this was not the same Job they had known. He was a broken man, and they sympathize momentarily. *"They sat down with him upon the ground seven days and seven nights and none spoke a word unto him; for they saw that his grief was very great."* (Job 2:13)

Picture this scene for yourself. You have severe circumstances come into your life. Your friends come calling and they sit and stare at you for seven days and seven nights. It would not be long before you, too, would begin to be aware of what a pitiful sight you are. Job now begins to react to his circumstances.

Job's words are recorded in Chapter 3:1-3, 20, 21. *"After this Job opened his mouth, and cursed his day. And Job spoke, and said, Let the day perish in which I was born, and the night in which it was said, There is a male child conceived Wherefore is light given to him that is in misery, and life unto the bitter in soul; Who long for death, but it cometh not, and dig for it more than for hidden treasures."*

Essentially Job says, "Let me forget that I'm even alive. I wish I were dead. I'd do anything rather than be in the state that I'm in. Oh, if I could just die!"

Have you ever felt like this? Have you cried out in the privacy of your own room or in some secret place (without any of your Christian friends hearing you, of course), "I wish I were dead! Everybody else seems so radiant and happy, but they don't have the problems I have?"

But soon you find yourself carrying on life as usual. You get your smile on, go to church or to some Christian meeting and cheerily say, "I'm just terrific. How are you?" As long as all the believers keep their "faces" on, then no one knows the heart of anyone else and the result is the loss of reality in Christ. Job did not fake it. He openly complained and expressed his needs and feelings. (Nevertheless God calls him one of the "greats" among saints. Ezekiel 14:14)

The first of Job's so-called comforters, Eliphaz the Temanite, speaks. *"Then Eliphaz, the Temanite, answered and said, If we venture to converse with thee, wilt thou be grieved? But who can withhold himself from speaking? Behold, thou hast instructed many, and thou hast strengthened the weak hands. Thy words have upheld him that was falling, and thou hast strengthened the feeble knees. But now it is come upon thee, and thou faintest; it toucheth thee, and thou are troubled. Remember, I pray thee, whoever perished, being innocent? Or where were the righteous cut off? Even as I have seen they that plow iniquity, and sow wickedness reap the same. By the blast of God they perish, and by the breath of his nostrils are they consumed."* (Job 4:1-5, 7-9)

Loosely translated, Eliphaz is saying, "Now Job, you know your Bible. You have helped a lot of people. You have taught the Truth; why you know that God wouldn't have allowed these things to happen to you if you didn't deserve it. There must be sin in your life. Are you truly yielded? You are simply reaping what you have sown. We all know that is the way God works!"

Eliphaz is mouthing the dogma of his day. "If you suffer it is a result of sin and failure. If everything is going well it is a sign that you have been good and God is blessing you." Notice the emphasis on *man* that is inherent in this thinking.

Today this same line of reasoning is pursued on every hand, even among those who claim to know the Scripture. How often we are told, "It all depends on *you*. God cannot work in your life *unless* you do these specific things."

What a weak God Who is thwarted on every hand by humans in order to carry out His plans! And how important man becomes in this. The result is humanism, which attempts to make God perform like a man. The God of the Bible is sovereign over all, even over the will of man. (Romans 9:19)

The generalizations of Eliphaz about being rewarded on the basis of iniquity would not have looked so convincing in light of God's word in Psalm 103:10, *"He hath not dealt with us after our sins, nor rewarded us according to our iniquities."*

His suggestion that the righteous are never cut off would be questionable in light of the state Christ left John the Baptist, in the New Testament. As you may recall, Christ said of John the Baptist, *"Among them that are born of women there hath not risen a greater than John the Baptist."* (Matthew 11:11a) Yet, the Lord left John to be beheaded at the hands of Herod.)

Or what about Jesus Himself who was innocent and righteous yet was cut off and *"tasted death?"* How much we need to relearn the truth of Isaiah 55:8, *"For my thoughts are not your thoughts, neither are your ways my ways, saith the Lord."*

After Eliphaz has analyzed Job's plight in terms of his traditional understanding, he proceeds to give Job advice. *"I would seek unto God,* (if I were you, Job) *and unto God would I commit my cause, who doeth great things and unsearchable, marvelous things without number... He shall deliver thee in six troubles; yea, in seven there shall no evil touch thee."* (Job 5:8, 9, 19.)

Superficially these statements of Eliphaz sound very comforting and very familiar. How often today we are told, or we tell others, that God "*is able to do exceedingly abundantly above all that we can ask or think.*" (Ephesians 3:20)

But let's be practical about the application of Eliphaz's statements. Did he actually think that God-honoring Job had not already sought God's face in these matters? The first thing that Job as a believer would have done in his trial was go to the Lord. He had already "committed his cause" to the Lord. ("*The Lord gave and the Lord hath taken away; blessed be the name of the Lord.*" Job 1:21b)

Secondly, Eliphaz states that once one commits his cause to the Lord, the Lord will deliver him. But, Job could have asked Eliphaz, "How soon will deliverance come? One day, two years, ten years?"

And Eliphaz seems to equate deliverance with a sign of God's blessing being restored. Yet has God anywhere said that in the *second* or the *minute* or the *day* that one looks to Him, He will instantaneously rearrange circumstances?

Finally, Eliphaz insults Job's understanding as a believer. He self-righteously quotes Bible verses at Job and judges Job to be "backslidden."

Job Argues His Own Case

Job answers Eliphaz in Chapter 6. *"But Job answered and said, For the arrows of the Almighty are within me, the poison of it drinketh up my spirit; the terrors of God do set*
themselves in array against me. Oh, that I might have my request, and that God would grant me the thing that I long for! Even that it would please God to destroy me; that he would let loose his hand and cut me off! Teach me, and I will hold my tongue; and cause me to understand that in which I have erred. How forcible are right words! But what doth your arguing reprove? Now, therefore, be content, look upon me; for it is evident unto you if I lie. Return, I pray you, let it not be iniquity; yea, return again, my righteousness is in it." Job 6:4, 8, 9, 24, 25, 28, 29.

Job's answer includes the fact that he is most miserable because in the midst of his trial he is not experiencing even God's comfort. He senses that what has come upon him is God's doing, yet he cannot understand it. The only thing that holds comfort for Job is the idea of dying.

To his friends he is very forthright. He asks them to specifically point out his sin since they seem so convinced that all his problems result from his personal sin or failure.

And in conclusion he answers their accusation with an amazing truth. He says, "You think God is dealing with me because of some iniquity in me. But, actually, He is working in my life because of my righteousness!"

What an interesting argument Job presents to his friends! And it is a Scriptural answer! *"For whom the Lord loveth he chasteneth and scourgeth every son whom he receiveth But if ye be without chastisement, of which all are partakers, then are ye bastards and not sons.*" (Hebrews 12:6, 8) God Himself had declared Job perfect (righteous, and therefore a son of God), and now Job simply states that whatever is happening in his life must have its explanation in the *fact* of his relationship with his Heavenly Father.

Are we this clear about the fact that our "righteousness" is the reason we are experiencing trials and tribulations in our lives? When we have come to know Christ as Savior, we have been clothed with His righteousness and have been brought into Sonship. This qualifies us for chastisement! The Lord will work His life in us and that process will be painful. For the joy that was set before Him, Jesus endured the cross. (Hebrews 12:4) Are we focused on the joy of being His and the awesome privilege of being trained up in Him?

Job Talks to the Father

Now Job turns his conversation to God Himself. He tells the Lord how confused and mystified he is with the events in his life.

In Chapter 7 he cries out to God, *"When I say, My bed shall comfort me, then thou scarest me with dreams and terrifiest me through visions."* He asks, *"What is man, that thou shouldest set thine heart upon him, and that thou shouldest visit him every morning, and test him every moment?"*

And finally he confesses the fact of his humanity, the failure of the flesh generally. *"I have sinned. What shall I do unto thee, O thou preserver of men? Why hast thou set me as a mark against thee, so that I am a burden to myself?"* Job never once forgets that as a human he really deserves nothing from God; yet, he knows that he has had a relationship with God in the past and even now he asserts his openness before the Lord. He tells God exactly how he feels.

In his conversation with the Lord, Job brings to light some wonderful truths about the nature of God. He has known that God is in charge of every detail in our lives including our sleeping time. Further he indicates that God is dealing with His children *every moment*, not just in the crisis!

Think about that. Do we really believe that God is working in us and in the details of everything that happens to us every minute of every day of our life?

Paul has said this in a little more general way in Philippians 1:6. *"Being confident of this very thing, that he who has begun a good work in you will perform it unto the day of Jesus Christ."* God is *continually* performing *His* good work in me! (Note, please, that there is no clause in that verse which makes His working dependent upon something that we do or fail to do. He is always and continuingly conforming us to the image of His Son.)

Finally, Job reminds God of His sovereignty as he refers to Him as *"thou preserver of men."* We can do nothing of ourselves. God is in charge of the lives of men.

We stated earlier that this was the "winter" of Job's growth and maturity. He has been complaining and murmuring. He has *not* been "claiming" I Thessalonians 5:18. *"In everything give thanks for this is the will of God in Christ Jesus concerning you."*

Yet, in the midst of Job's trials and complaints, wonderful growth is in progress. He is being pushed to God alone as his Source of Wisdom. His friends' platitudes are far too unsatisfying.

Further, Job will discover that God's ways are not always logical, based upon man's way of thinking. He is discovering more and more about the grace of God as He, the Heavenly Father, allows Job to come to Him boldly with his complaints, his confusion and his desperation.

Bildad Adds His "Two Cents" Worth

Job's second so-called comforter, Bildad, now steps up to give his wisdom in Chapter 8. It seems that he is singing the same song, second verse, of what Eliphaz has just sung. He says, *"If thou wert pure and upright, surely now he would awake for thee, and make the habitation of thy righteousness prosperous. For inquire I pray thee, of the former age, and prepare thyself to the search of their fathers; Behold, God will not cast away a perfect man, neither will he help the evildoers."* Job 8:6, 8, 20.

Bildad essentially tells Job that the fault is Job's. Whatever has befallen Job is a result of sin and failure in Job's life, so says Bildad. Further, Bildad calls upon the *"fathers"* for support in verse eight. He says that even tradition tells Job that this is true.

Finally, Bildad makes the sweeping statement that God will not cast away anyone who is perfect, inferring that Job is not perfect and leaving the unspoken suggestion that he, Bildad, must be since nothing horrible is presently happening to him.

How often have we taken this position toward friends or relatives who are going through difficult times? Or, perhaps we have experienced this kind of judgment from other believers who are living in the tradition of the *"fathers."*

Job's reply is amazingly perceptive. He says, "*I know it is so of a truth; but how should man be just before God?*" (Job 9:1) Job tells Bildad that he agrees that this is the traditional theological teaching. However, Job identifies some holes in the traditional theories. Essentially Job is asking, "How good do I have to be to be good enough to get God's blessing?"

Later in the chapter Job goes on to point out that even if he could justify himself before God the very act of justifying himself would show pride or self-righteousness and he would be back in the trap of sin and imperfection. (Job 9:20, 21)

Further, Job points out that God alone is in control of what happens in his life and though he, Job, might seem to be living above sin, God could allow him to drop into sin at any moment. (Job 9:30, 31)

In Chapter 10 Job pursues this reasoning and points out that God is truly the One in control of all of life. He is Job's Creator and Sustainer.

Job has raised the question that all of organized Christianity needs to be honestly answering. "Is there a level of performance which man can attain which will then earn him God's blessing?" In Job's own words, "*But how should man be just before God?*"

Perhaps we should ask this question every time a speaker or a preacher exhorts true believers with these words, "Simply commit your life, yield yourself unto God and He will bless you."

How committed is committed enough? What if we just gossip a little today, but don't get drunk? Does that mean that God will bless us more because we only gossiped? Or, must we be absolutely sinless without even a sinful thought before God can bless us? And if the latter is true, how long can we go before the first evil thought enters our mind? And when that first sinful thought comes, how long is it before God removes the blessing that He has hardly had time to bestow?

In other words, how clean is clean? How will we know when we have attained the required level of yieldedness? Some of the church *"fathers"* of the more recent past could have born the name of Bildad, as he stated, *"If thou were pure and upright."*

Even David of the Old Testament did not find God to be this kind of a man-like judge. In his own life David discovered that God *"hath not dealt with us after our sins, nor rewarded us according to our iniquities. For as the heavens are high above the earth, so great is his mercy toward them that fear him."* (Psalms 103:10, 11)

In Chapter 10 Job speaks boldly to the Lord Himself and claims that he is not wicked. (Job 10:7) Further he reminds God that he was simply clay and God Himself was the One Who had made him as he was. Job knew, in the depth of his being, that God had accepted him as perfect and righteous, yet he could see his own humanity and failure and cried, *"I am full of confusion."* (Job 10:25)

Confusion and fear often go together for us as believers. The word of God states that *"God has not given us a spirit of fear, but of power, love and a sound mind."* (2 Timothy 1:7). When we are confused, we know that we are not walking by faith. We then begin to experience such discomfort that we are pressed into the realm of the Spirit because we call on the name of the Lord in our desperation!

Herein is the secret purpose of suffering. The Lord is teaching us how to access the kingdom of His dear Son and transfer out of the realm of the flesh. The practical process is that of calling upon Him. *"Whosoever calleth upon the name of the Lord shall be saved."* (Romans 10:23)

In our humanness we do not call initially. We rather complain, whine, wallow in self-pity, proclaim our innocence, cogitate, plan and analyze. However, God is asking us to look upon Him by faith and call upon His name! And, He is revealing His character to us, letting us know he is sovereign over all.

Zophar Adds More Dogma

Job's third "friend" and "counselor" steps forward now and mocks Job's words: *"For thou hast said, My doctrine is pure, and I am clean in thine eyes. But, oh, that God would speak, and open his lips against thee."* (Job 11:4, 5)

Zophar goes on to sing the third verse of the original tune, *"If iniquity be in thine hand, put it far away, and let not wickedness dwell in thy tents. For then shalt thou lift up thy face without spot; yea, thou shalt be steadfast, and shalt not fear; But the eyes of the wicked shall fail, and they shall not escape, and their hope shall be as one dying."* (Job 11:14, 15, 20)

Isn't it interesting that Job's three friends all have the same outlook, the same dogma, the same view of God and the Scripture? Job must have begun to wonder if his understanding of the Lord was wrong. Perhaps he began to wonder if his faith and trust in God's love and faithfulness were misplaced.

Today the largest part of Christendom holds the humanistic philosophy that matches that of Job's so-called friends. As a result, when we as believers dare to cast ourselves fully upon the Lord, giving Him all our sins, failures, confusions and concerns, we often run into many Christian friends who question our sanity and our theology. They want us to simply "shape up." This was the very kind of message Job was receiving from his religious friends.

Be not dismayed. This act of utter faith is the essence of what God is doing in our lives. He is bringing us to the end of ourselves, again and again. We are to cast our burdens upon Him and believe that He is able to keep us from

58

falling and present us blameless before the throne of grace! (See Jude 24.)

In Chapters 12, 13 and 14 Job presents his own thoughts about his dilemma. Throughout his monologue, touches of sarcasm appear as he speaks to the three friends. He begins, *"No doubt but ye are the people, and wisdom shall die with you."* (Job 12:1)

Are there not Christian leaders today who would lead us to believe that they know all the truth, failing to recognize that if this were so they would be God Himself? The impression is so often conveyed by some that they have the Truth and surely if they die, Truth will be lost forever. There is very little thought given to the fact that the Scripture indicates that the Holy Spirit is the Teacher of every believer and He can get the job done without the help of man! (I John 2:27)

What a wonderful peace there is when we discover that God is faithful, and He will accomplish His plan in spite of apostates or heretics. It was this sure knowledge that allowed the Apostle Paul to write,

"And many of the brethren in the Lord, becoming confident by my bonds, are much more bold to speak the word without fear. Some indeed, preach Christ even of envy and strife; and some also of good will; The one preach Christ out of contention, not sincerely, supposing to add affliction to my bonds; But the other of love, knowing that I am set for the defense of the gospel. What then? Notwithstanding, every way, whether in pretense or in truth, Christ is preached; and in that I do rejoice, yea, and will rejoice." (Philippians 1:14-18)

Job's rebuttal continues, *"But I have understanding as well as you; I am not inferior to you; yea, who knoweth not such things as these?*" He points out that he is not a spiritual dummy. He is familiar with what they are saying, but what they are saying simply does not apply in his situation. In fact, the incessant folly of their remarks drives Job to cry out, *"Surely I would speak to the Almighty, and I desire to reason with God."*

This cry marks a high point in the growth process as it is at work in Job. He has come to the end of himself; he has found no comfort in friends; familiar dogma has been found wanting; he will be satisfied with nothing less than God's own answer in his life.

Perhaps some of us can identify with Job. We have listened too long to the opinions of mere humans as they have explained God to us. Conference after conference, speaker after speaker, book after book, leave something to be desired. We ache with the desire of Paul, *"That I may know Him, and the power of his resurrection, and the fellowship of his sufferings, being made conformable unto his death."* (Philippians 3:10) May the Spirit of God bring each of us to this stage of growth.

Even as Job considers this personal conversation with God, his mind turns to the very character of God, as he has known him in years past. And Job triumphantly declares, *"Though he slay me, yet will I trust in him."* (Job 13:15a) Here in the very heart of his struggle Job has been given the grace and the understanding to hang on through the struggle. He can say, "I don't understand what you're doing, Lord, but I believe that I can trust you."

What a truth for us to apply personally. When God takes us through the hard places, the season of suffering, He gives us grace for the dark spots. We may feel that we will not last another moment because of the pain or the pressure or the sorrow or the confusion. Yet we are being given the strength to endure even in that very moment in which we are crying out. In these lonely places we learn the most about Him whom we desire to know and that is the purpose of God in our lives! He is conforming us to His image!

As Job recalls afresh how utterly dependent he is upon God for his very life, his mind races into a consideration of the sovereignty of God in every area.

In Chapter 14 he says, *"Who can bring a clean thing out of unclean? Not one."* (Job 14:4) In other words, man born of a human cannot enter the world sinless; it is impossible. The conclusion then must be that only God could make a man acceptable, clean and perfect.

Further, Job says that man's *"days are determined. The number of his months are with thee, thou hast appointed his bounds that he cannot pass."* (Job 14:5) Amazing truth! Job flatly declares that God has determined the days of every man. No individual will step outside the boundaries that the sovereign God has set. In fact, Job goes on to state that our very steps are numbered by God. (Job 14:16)

The wise King Solomon knew these truths about a sovereign God. We read in Proverbs 16:9, *"A man's heart deviseth his way, but the Lord directeth his steps."* King David tells us that all our days are written beforehand in a book! (Psalm 139:16)

Many New Testament passages support these same truths, so they cannot be passed off by some "higher critic" who would say, "That is just Job talking. That is not the actual truth about God." In Hebrews 9:27 we read, *"And as it is appointed unto men once to die."* We will die on God's *appointed* day and time.

Jesus underscores the sovereignty of the Father as He teaches in Matthew 6:27, *"which of you being anxious can add one cubit unto his stature?"* or Matthew 10:29-31, *"Are not two sparrows sold for a farthing? And one of them shall not fall on the ground without your Father. But the very hairs of your head are all numbered. Fear not, therefore; ye are of more value than many sparrows."* Finally we read of God *"who worketh all things after the counsel of his own will."* (Ephesians 1:11b)

These truths go against the grain of much of the dogma within the organized church of today. We hear so much about man's free will. We are given the humanistic logic that God has created us with a free will, and therefore He has allowed us to go our own way, doing things which He never meant to have happen. We are taught that many of our actions are "outside His best plan for us" because He will not infringe upon our freedom of choice.

The word of God teaches absolutely the opposite. In Romans 8:7 we read, *"The carnal mind is enmity against God; for it is not subject to the law of God, neither, indeed can be."* Man is totally depraved before he comes to Jesus Christ and he cannot choose good. This is confirmed in Romans 7:18, *"For I know that in me (that is, in my flesh) dwelleth no good thing; for to will is present with me, but how to perform that which is good I find not."* I am not even free to choose Jesus Christ; He must choose me. *"Ye have not chosen me; but I have chosen you."* (John 15:16b) *"No man can come to me, except the Father, who hath sent me, draw him; and I will raise him up at the last day."* (John 6:44) And, further, if Christ chooses a man that person cannot resist this inward call of the Holy Spirit. *"For who hath resisted his will?"* (Romans 9:19b) *"All that the Father giveth me shall come to me."* (John 6:37)

Even after a person receives the gift of eternal life and the Spirit of God lives within, he or she is not able or capable under his or her own power or ability to produce that which is good. When the believer exercises his will and chooses that which is good in God's eyes, the choice is a result of the action of the Holy Spirit in his life. *"For it is God who worketh in you both to will and to do of his good pleasure."* (Philippians 2:13) *"Not that we are sufficient of ourselves to think anything as of ourselves, but our sufficiency is of God."* (II Corinthians 3:5)

Job is discovering the reality of these truths in depth. This very discovery and understanding is a vital part of growth. It is a method of maturity in the life of every believer, and the Spirit is the One who gives understanding.

CHAPTER FOUR

CLAY BECOMES GOLD

In the science of geology, men have discovered that pressure applied over long periods of time produces precious stones out of the substance of the earth. God's methods in the lives of believers are very similar. We are clay in His hands, yet He speaks of us as His jewels, His precious stones. "*... chosen of God and precious, ye also, as living stones, are built up a spiritual house, an holy priesthood, to offer up spiritual sacrifices, acceptable to God by Jesus Christ.*" (I Peter 2:4b, 5) "*And they shall be mine, saith the Lord of hosts, in that day when I make up my jewels; and I will spare them as a man spareth his own son that serveth him!*" (Malachi 3:17)

To continue the analogy, diamonds are not taken in their rough state, directly from the earth, and placed on a piece of black velvet in the display case. Instead the rock is taken into the workshop to be pounded, cut and polished several times.

God does not call us to Himself and then say, "Now you simply sit back, watch television and eat chocolates because from here on into heaven the road is an easy one." No, He essentially says, "Now you are mine, yet in the rough stage. But I am going to change you into a beautiful jewel. In fact there will not be another jewel like you in my jewel collection. But this change will take some time; it will require some painful work and circumstances. Yet in the midst of the pounding, cutting and polishing you may be assured that I love you. I hand-picked you from the clay around you."

Every believer passes through the periods of pressure, moving from clay to precious stone and then on into the period of "pounding, cutting and polishing." Someone has even said that a goldsmith polishes the gold until he can see his own image in its surface. And so those whom the Lord foreknew, *"...he also did predestinate to be conformed to the image of his Son."* (Romans 8:29a)

Thus, God is polishing His righteous servant Job. The pressure increases in Job's life, as is evident in Chapters 13 through 37. The accusations of his friends become more vehement. Eventually Elihee, a distant relative, adds further condemnation.

🐦   Eliphaz becomes almost sarcastic and slanderous in his statements to Job now: *"For thy mouth uttereth thine iniquity, and thou chooses the tongue of the crafty. What knowest thou, that we know not? What understandest thou, which is not in us? With us are both the grayheaded and very aged men, much older than thy father. Why doth thine heart carry thee away? And what do thine eyes wink at, that thou turnest thy spirit against God, and lettest such words go out of thy mouth? The wicked man travaileth with pain all his days, and the number of years is hidden to the oppressor. A dreadful sound is in his ears; in prosperity the destroyer shall come upon him. It shall be accomplished before his time, and his branch shall not be green."* (Job 15:2, 9, 10, 12, 13, 20, 21, 32)

First, Job's friend accuses him of a "crafty" tongue, assuming then that Job is cleverly concealing his sin. Further Eliphaz points out that tradition is on the side of the argument that he and his friends are presenting to Job. Then he judges that Job has turned against God based on the fact that Job has boldly questioned God's activities in his life. Eliphaz and the others place the blame for Job's dilemma squarely on Job. Yet Job has maintained that God is in control of all that is happening.

Finally Eliphaz says that the *"destroyer shall come"* upon the *"wicked man"* when the man is *"in prosperity."* Therefore, he concludes, Job is a very wicked man. He does not see any greenery on Job's branches! He is judging by outward appearance and the tradition of men.

Job Has a Few Words Himself

Job answers Eliphaz with some interesting points. *"I also could speak as ye do: if your soul were in my soul's stead. I could heap up words against you, and shake mine head at you. But I would strengthen you with my mouth, and the moving of my lips should assuage your grief. My face is foul with weeping, and on my eyelids is the shadow of death; not for any violence in mine hands. Also my prayer is pure. Also, now, behold, my witness is in heaven, and my record is on high."* (Job 16:4, 5, 16, 17, 19)

Job says that it is always easy to judge another person in whose situation you are not and have not been. But, he goes on to say that he would be a comforter to them if they were in his place.

Job's words are similar to the experience of Paul as the Apostle discovered God's grace through suffering. He spoke of *"...the God of all comfort, who comforteth us in all our tribulation, that we may be able to comfort them who are in any trouble, by the comfort with which we ourselves are comforted of God. For as the sufferings of Christ abound in us, so our consolation also aboundeth by Christ."* (II Corinthians 1:3b-5)

Further, Job answers the accusation that he is a wicked man who is in rebellion against God. He points out that he has shed many tears of concern before the Lord and that his prayer life is open and pure before God. (Who can know the agony of a believer before the Lord over some failure or sin or confusion in his or her life?)

And Job claims God as his witness that he is righteous and acceptable before the Lord. He is standing on the solid ground that is available to every believer, no matter what his circumstances or his life condition. As Paul writes, *"Who shall lay any thing to the charge of God's elect? Shall God that justifieth? Who is he that condemneth? Shall Christ that died, yea rather, that is risen again, who is even at the right hand of God who also maketh intercession for us?"* (Romans 8:32, 33) Job is not justifying himself before his friends on the grounds of his "perfect" humanity but rather because he knows that he has a relationship with his Heavenly Father. He has been declared righteous by God's grace.

When we suffer and experience failures, trials, temptations and tragedies, we tend to blame ourselves as if that is a demonstration of repentance or humility. Often our friends, like Job's friends, wonder where we have gone astray and what we can do to prevent ongoing problems in our lives. But Job does not look at himself or his failure! Rather, he actually proclaims his faith. He says that he is looking by faith to his "witness in heaven" i.e. his Redeemer. (Job 16: 19; 19:25-27). He also says that his attitude toward Eliphaz, if the tables were turned, would be that of being a comforter rather than one who condemns (Job 16:5).

Obviously Job has learned the principles of grace. He has seen his own failure and knows the Lord as the God of mercy. (Job 13:3,6,7,8,18) This is the life of faith.

Bildad Adds "Two Cents" More

Bildad becomes rather heated in the discussion now. He says, *"Shall the earth be forsaken for thee? Yea, the light of the wicked shall be put out, and the spark of his fire shall not shine. Brimstone shall be scattered upon his habitation. He shall have neither son nor nephew among his people. Surely such are the dwellings of the wicked, and this is the place of him that knoweth not God."* (Job 18:4, 5, 15, 19, 21)

Bildad stressed the fact that Job is certainly no one special. God has always punished the wicked; Job will be no exception. And Bildad insinuates that Job is among those that *"knoweth not God."* Here is a religionist who judges on outward appearances and worldly reasonings. He has judged Job on the basis of his own human knowledge of the reward system.

⬛ *"Then Job answered and said, How long will ye vex my soul, and break me in pieces with words? My kinsfolk have failed, and my familiar friends have forgotten me All my inward friends abhorred me, and they whom I loved are turned against me. Have pity upon me, have pity upon me, O ye my friends, for the hand of God hath touched me. For I know that my redeemer liveth and that he shall stand at the latter day upon the earth; and though after my skin worms destroy this body, yet in my flesh shall I see God."* (Job 19:1, 2, 14, 19, 21, 25, 26)

What a tremendous picture of the steps God uses in a man's life to bring him to new measures of faith! The circumstances of Job's life caused him to become an outcast to some. Then his friends became his accusers. And these are the pressures that drove him to God and God alone. And his discovery is one of the high points of the Old Testament. Job states, *"I know that my redeemer liveth and in my flesh shall I see God."* He has so grown in the knowledge of the Redeemer that he truly knows something of the *"power of the resurrection."* And he has been learning much about the *"fellowship of His sufferings."* (Philippians 3:10)

As objective observers we might have been tempted to feel very sorry for Job, especially as we view the treatment his friends gave him. Yet the great truth that *"all things work together for good to them that love God, to them who are the called according to his purpose"* is very evident in the life of Job. (Romans 8:28) With Joseph of old, Job could say, *"But as for you, ye thought evil against me, but God meant it unto good"* Genesis 50:20a) Is this the confession that springs from our mouths when trouble comes? Or do we whine and complain about our circumstances?

71

In Chapter 20 Zophar gets in a final word by reminding Job again of the terrible punishments which befall the wicked. Job replies in Chapter 21 by reminding Zophar that there are plenty of wicked people who are prospering; all Zophar needs to do is take a look around him. So, Job suggests that there must be some area of falsehood in Zophar's maxim.

Eliphaz returns for a concluding word also. He exhorts Job to *"return to the Almighty"* and then his life will be put back in order. Job answers with a statement of faith. In Job 23:10-14 he says: *"But he knoweth the way that I take; when he hath tested me, I shall come forth as gold. My foot hath held his steps, his way have I kept and not declined. Neither have I gone back from the commandment of his lips; I have esteemed the words of his mouth more than my necessary food. But he is of one mind, and who can turn him? And what his soul desireth, even that he doeth. For he performeth the thing that is appointed for me; and many such things are with him."*

Job asserts the fact that he already is walking with the Lord. He perceives that this trial is a process of refining which his Sovereign Lord is taking him through. Further, Job proclaims that the end result will be good, pure gold.

Job also proclaims the fact that man does not change God's mind. God will carry out His own will; He will not be turned or thwarted by a human. He will perform those things that He has appointed before the foundation of the world.

The Word of God substantiates Job's understanding at every turn. *"And all the inhabitants of the earth are reputed as nothing; and he doeth according to his will in the army of heaven, and among the inhabitants of the earth, and none can stay his hand, or say unto him, What doest thou?"* (Daniel 4:35)

Notice where Job turns time after time for refuge and comfort. He counts on the sovereignty of God. There is no firmer foundation for practical living than the fact that the God who loves us is completely in charge of our past, present and future. He is creating His jewels and our response is to be one of praise and trust.

Bildad reappears with a final question for Job. *"How then can man be justified with God? Or how then can he be clean that is born of a woman? Behold even to the moon, and it shineth not; yea, the stars are not pure in his sight. How much less man, who is a worm; and the son of man, who is a worm?"* (Job 25:4-6)

Job answers Bildad by first maintaining his own righteousness. *"My righteousness I hold fast, and will not let it go; my heart shall not reproach me as long as I live."* (Job 27:6) However, Job goes on to say that the wisdom that would reconcile his apparent "punishment" at God's hands and his simultaneous assurance of right standing rest with God alone. *"Whence, then, cometh wisdom? And where is the place of understanding? God understandeth its way, and he knoweth the place of it."* (Job 28:20, 23) As for a human to have wisdom in these deep things, Job simply quotes God Himself. *"And unto man, He said, Behold, the fear of the Lord, that is wisdom; and to depart from evil is understanding."*

Finally Job laments over his current state of affairs and recalls happier days: *"Oh, that I were as in months past, as in the days when God preserved me; When his lamp shined upon my head, and when by his light I walked through darkness; As I was in the days of my youth, when the secret of God was upon my tent; When the Almighty was yet with me, when my children were about me; When I washed my steps with butter, and the rock poured me out rivers of oil; Then I said, I shall die in my nest, and I shall multiply my days as the sand My glory was fresh in me, and my bow was renewed in my hand. Unto me men gave ear, and waited, and kept silence at my counsel. After my words they spoke not again; and my speech dropped upon them. And they waited for me as for the rain; and they opened their mouth wide as for the latter rain. I smiled on them when they had no confidence; and the light of countenance they cast not down.*" (Job 29:2-6, 18, 20-24)

"*But now they that are younger than I hold me in derision. And now my soul is poured out upon me; the days of affliction have taken hold upon me. I cry unto thee, and thou dost not hear me; I stand up, and thou regardest me not. When I looked for good, then evil came unto me; and when I waited for the light there came darkness. My heart was in turmoil, and rested not; the days of affliction came upon me.*" (Job 30:1a, 16, 20, 26, 27)

Job's cry is one that springs from the heart of God's children everywhere to some degree and at some point in each life. How often in days or months of spiritual dryness or spiritual weakness we recall past days when God "was really using us." Everything in life seemed rosy and we were experiencing God at work in us. Those around us could see it, and they commented often about our commitment to Him. They even sought us out when they needed prayer or when they simply wanted a "spiritual shot-in-the-arm."

But then came dark days when nothing seemed right. We could see our failures on every hand. Circumstances seemed to even work against us. Prayer didn't seem to change the situation. And we began to ask, "Where are you, Lord?"

Job has here simply described what he is feeling in the midst of his situation. What a tremendous opportunity for identification with him: we can be comforted in the midst of our own darkness especially as we see the conclusion of these dark days in Job's life.

Job Has Relatives, Too

According to Genesis 22:21, the Uzites and Buzites (Job and Elihu's family names) were close relatives. And, after Job's friends finished with him, his relative appears to plague Job further.

Elihu's anger had been kindled against Job because Job *"justified himself rather than God."* (Job 32:2b) Elihu was also angry with Job's three friends because *"they had found no answer, and yet had condemned Job."* (Job 32:3b)

Elihu's counsel is not much superior to that of Job's three friends. He, too, condemns Job without giving him an answer or any comfort. The first three counselors had agreed among themselves that Job was secretly guilty of sin. Elihu is not as concerned with any secret sin of Job's as he is with Job's attitude. Elihu feels that Job as a human has absolutely no right to ask questions of God nor to suggest that God may be treating him unfairly. Elihu's comments include:

"Behold, in this thou are not just; I will answer thee, that God is greater than man. Why dost thou strive against him? For he giveth not account of any of his matters." (Job 33:12, 13)

"Behold, God exalteth by his power; who teacheth like him? Who hath directed him his way? Or who can say, Thou has wrought iniquity? Remember that thou magnify his work, which men behold. Every man may see it; many may behold it afar off. Behold, God is great, and we know him not, neither can the number of his years be searched out." (Job 36:22-26)

"God thundereth marvelously with his voice; great things doeth he which we cannot comprehend." (Job 37:5)

Elihu's views of God are commendable and he builds a wonderful case for the righteousness and sovereignty of God. But Job might well have asked of him, *"Will ye contend for God?"* (Job 13:8b) Surely God does not need a human to come to his defense. Elihu only adds to the human condemnation that Job is already suffering.

Interestingly enough, Elihu attacks the very foundation of Job's faith in the sovereign wisdom of God. Elihu virtually says that if Job really understood God's sovereignty he wouldn't think of having these confused feelings! Once again Elihu tempts Job to focus on himself and his apparent failure, based on Elihu's human evaluation of the situation. The reality is that Job knows that the Lord cares for him completely and in that security knows he is free to express his human feelings.

CHAPTER FIVE

JOB MEETS HIS MAKER

Helmut Thielicke has written:

"Christ bears to Our Father the most severe and constricting anxiety which we undergo when we can no longer see the hand of the Father in what befalls us. For it is true, is it not, that we can put up with even the worst things so long as we can accept them in the sense of seeing meaning in them, of detecting the high thoughts of God concerning them?" 4

It was this kind of "severe and constricting anxiety" which Job has suffered throughout the book. He longed to understand what God was doing in his life. Yet he felt forsaken and persecuted. *"For the arrows of the Almighty are within me, the poison of it drinketh up my spirit." (Job 6:4a) "Surely I would speak to the Almighty and I desire to reason with God." (Job 13:3)*

Job had experienced a relationship with the Lord in earlier days (Job 1:1-6), yet now his faith appears to be wavering a bit. Confusion, questioning and frustration have set in. How much Job needed to be comforted with the truth from passages like Hebrews 12:2 where the Redeemer is described as the *"author and finisher of our faith."* Job needed to be encouraged by the promise that the God who had planted in him the faith to believe would also continue to supply and bring that faith to completion. Job needed to know that he could have confidence in *"this very thing, that He who hath begun a good work in you will perform it until the day of Jesus Christ."* (Philippians 1:6)

God Meets Job In His Desperation

God has promised that He will not allow us to be tried beyond that which we can endure, (I Corinthians 10:13), and in His wisdom He comes to Job personally. The Lord appears just after Elihu's flowery speech concerning God's inscrutability.

Elihu had suggested that Job was out of line to think that God should converse with him. (Job 35: 5-8) The fact that the Lord speaks at this point seems to be a direct refutation of Elihu's counsel.

"Then the Lord answered Job out of the whirlwind and said, Who is this that darkeneth counsel by words without knowledge? Where was thou when I laid the foundations of the earth? Declare, if thou hast understanding. Where is the way where light dwelleth? And as for darkness, where is its place, that thou shouldest take it to its domain, and that thou shouldest know the paths to its house? Knowest thou it, because thou wast then born, or because the number of thy days is great? Knowest thou the ordinances of heaven? Canst thou set its dominion in the earth? Who hath put wisdom in the inward parts? Or who hath given understanding to the heart? " (Job 38:1, 2, 4, 19, 20, 21, 33, 36)

"Hast thou given the horse strength? Hast thou clothed his neck with thunder? Doth the hawk fly by thy wisdom, and stretch her wings toward the south? Doth the eagle mount up at thy command, and make her nest on high?" (Job 39:19, 26, 27)

"Moreover, the Lord answered Job, and said, Shall he that contendeth with the Almighty instruct him? He that reproveth God, let him answer it." (Job 40:1, 2)

What an experience for Job! He has been in the darkness, feeling absolutely forsaken by the Father; and suddenly he is honored by the blazing majesty of God Himself. Think of that! To know God through this personal confrontation with Him after such a prolonged period of seeming separation must have been a shocking relief!

The Lord's words to Job are continuing revelations of His sovereignty – His invincible power. He has not answered any of Job's specific queries. Job's response is very brief and very fitting for a human in the presence of his Creator: *"Then Job answered the Lord, and said, Behold, I am vile; what shall I answer thee? I will lay mine hand upon my mouth. Once have I spoken, but I will not answer; yea, twice, but I will proceed no further."* (Job 40:3-5)

Job is so in awe of God's presence, His majesty, His wisdom, that he is not aware of his unanswered questions. He is only conscious of his own vileness, his unworthiness, his humanity.

The Lord continues to reveal Himself to Job: *"Wilt thou also annul my judgment? Wilt thou condemn me, that thou mayest be justified? Hast thou an arm like God? Or canst thou thunder with a voice like him? Deck thyself now with majesty and excellency; and array thyself with glory and beauty. Cast abroad the rage of thy wrath; and behold everyone that is proud, and abase him. Look on everyone that is proud, and bring him low; and tread down the wicked in their place. Hide them in the dust together, and bind their faces in secret. Then will I also confess unto thee that thine own right hand can save thee."* (Job 40:8-14)

The Lord portrays to Job his lack of power as a human, his inability to control circumstances or people. He says, Job, if you have my strength, if you can speak with my voice, if you can produce your own majesty, if you can humble the proud and judge the wicked; then I will concede that you can save yourself.

Essentially God reveals to Job that he is in no way the "master of his own fate" or the "captain of his own soul." Rather, all that happens is within God's control – not the control of any human.

Job's second response indicates what he is discovering about the character of the Father:
"Then Job answered the Lord, and said, I know that thou canst do everything, and that no thought can be withheld from thee. Who is he who hideth counsel without knowledge? Therefore have I uttered that which I understood not; things too wonderful for me, which I knew not. Hear, I beseech thee, and I will speak; I will demand of thee, and declare thou unto me. I have heard of thee by the hearing of the ear, but now mine eye seeth thee. Wherefore I abhor myself, and repent in dust and ashes." (Job 42: 1-6)

Job responds by agreeing that he is guilty of that which God has said about him. He has spoken *"words without knowledge."* (Job 38:2) He has assumed that it was his prerogative to know what God was doing in his life. He has discovered with the Psalmist, *"Such knowledge is too wonderful for me, it is high, I cannot attain unto it."* (Psalm 139:6)

This is the peak, the climax, of the Book of Job. It is also the ultimate in human knowledge about God Himself. Job has understood by experience the truth that God has spoken. *"For my thoughts are not your thoughts, neither are your ways my ways...For as the heavens are higher than the earth, so are my ways higher than your ways, and my thoughts than your thoughts."* (Isaiah 55:8, 9)

If Job, or any human, could fully understand God's ways or even God Himself, that person would have to be God. Thus, our part as humans is to trust Him implicitly. We are brought to the place in our maturing as believers that we no longer have to understand our situations, but only to know the trustworthiness of our Father, Who has all things in His hand.

The Christian Hebraist A.S. Peake, in his commentary on Job (The Century Bible) summarizes the supreme lesson of the Book of Job as follows:
"His previous knowledge of God was that given by the traditional theology, in which he had been trained. It left no room for the suffering of the righteous, if the righteous suffered, then the theology was false. Such an inference Job had been forced to draw. But now he has seen God, and all is changed. He knows that God is righteous also. How these apparent contradictories can be intellectually reconciled he does not know. But he and God are again at one, a deeper fellowship is possible, untroubled by misgivings as to moral integrity. Happy, even in pain, that he has found himself and his God, he would rather suffer, if God willed it, than be in health and prosperity. He knows that all is well, he and his sufferings have their place in God's inscrutable design; why should he seek to understand it? In child-like reverence, he acknowledges it to be far beyond him. This mystical solution is the most precious thing the Book has to offer us." 5

In the midst of this "mystical solution" we come to "*know Him and the power of his resurrection.*" (Philippians 3:10) One of the characteristics of the Lord, then, is His sovereign inscrutability in some areas. Thus Paul could write with fervor:

"*What shall we say then? Is there unrighteousness with God? God forbid. For he saith to Moses, I will have mercy on whom I will have mercy, and I will have compassion on whom I will have compassion. So, then, it is not of him that willeth, nor of him that runneth, but of God that showeth mercy. For the scripture saith unto Pharaoh, Even for this same purpose have I raised thee up, that I might show my power in thee, and that my name might be declared throughout all the earth. Therefore hath he mercy on whom he will have mercy, and whom he will he hardeneth. Thou wilt say then unto me, Why doth he yet find fault? For who hath resisted His will? Nay but, O man, who art thou that repliest against God? Shall the thing formed say to him that formed it, Why hast thou made me thus? Hath not the potter power over the clay, of the same lump to make one vessel unto honour; and another unto dishonour.*" (Romans 9:14-21)

When the Holy Spirit has taught us this truth about the Father, we begin to see the possibility, the reality, of living a life of genuine peace, long-suffering and faith. We are by experience hiding in the Rock, fully knowing that "*The battle is the Lord's.*" (2 Chronicles 20:15) We are able then to fully trust Him whom we have discovered truly does "*work all things after the counsel of His own will.*" (Ephesians 1:11)

CHAPTER SIX

THE RICHES OF RIGHTEOUSNESS

Early in Job's conversations with his friends he stated that God was working in his life not because of hidden sin but actually because of Job's righteousness. *"Return, I pray you, let it not be iniquity; yea, return again, my righteousness is in it."* (Job 6:29)

As was pointed out earlier, Job's righteousness has come as a result of a faith-relationship with his Creator. He had "believed God" in whatever revelation God had given him about Himself. Thus, deep in his heart, Job knew God was dealing with him as His own child. The closing verses of Chapter 42 confirm this supposition.

⠐🐑   The Lord now directs some comments to those around Job: "*And it was, that after the Lord had spoken these words unto Job, the Lord said to Eliphaz, the Temanite, My wrath is kindled against thee, and against thy two friends; for ye have not spoken of me the thing that is right, as my servant Job hath. Therefore, take unto you now seven bullocks and seven rams, and go to my servant, Job, and offer up for yourselves a burnt offering. And my servant, Job, shall pray for you; for him will I accept; lest I deal with you after your folly, in that ye have not spoken of me the thing which is right, like my servant, Job. So Eliphaz, the Temanite, and Bildad, the Shuhite, and Zophar, the Naamathite, went, and did according as the Lord commanded them; the Lord also accepted Job.*" (Job 42:7-9)

God clearly condemns the dogma that Job's friends have been belaboring for months. "*Ye have not spoken of me the thing that is right.*" (Job 42:7) Secondly, He upholds the limited wisdom that Job had clung to in his own defense before his friends. The Lord says that Job has spoken that which was right about Himself. (Remember, God gave Job further revelation about Himself in the end, but He did not say that Job's statements were wrong.)

There is almost an ironic twist to the Lord's words to the friends. He basically says, "You better be thankful that righteous Job can intercede in your behalf or I would consider treating you in the foolish manner which you ascribed to me rewarding you after your iniquities!"

God Restores Job's Riches

The restoration of Job came in a series of steps. In Job 42:10a we read, *"and the Lord turned the captivity of Job."* By whom was Job taken captive? Satan. (Job 2:6) Who had delivered him to Satan? God. (Job 2:6) Who freed him from Satan's hold? The Lord Himself. (Job 42:10a)

Spiritual richness is ours as we are delivered out of the sphere of Satan's influence. Only the power of God can "turn our captivity." And, as in the life of Job, He will deliver the righteous in His own time and in His own way. *"But the Lord is faithful, who shall establish you, and keep you from evil."* (II Thessalonians 3:3) Like Job we must discover that there is a process involved in God's establishing and keeping us. That process includes time and suffering.

In Job 42:10b we read, *"Also the Lord gave Job twice as much as he had before."* Material blessing is once again Job's lot. And this time he is doubly blessed in the financial realm. What a gracious God! In writing about the righteous ones, those individuals justified by Christ's work upon the cross, Paul said, *"What shall we then say to these things? If God be for us, who can be against us? He that spared not his own Son, but delivered him up for us all, how shall he not with him also freely give us all things?"* (Romans 8:31, 32)

The Father delights in giving to His own.

"Then came there unto him all his brethren, and all his sisters, and all they that had been of his acquaintance before, and did eat bread with him in his house, and they bemoaned him, and comforted him over all the evil that the Lord had brought upon him. Every man also gave him a

piece of money, and every one an earring of gold." (Job 42:11)

What an emotional blessing this restoration must have been for Job! Remember his cry from his wretched state, *"My kinsfolk have failed, and my familiar friends have forgotten me."* (Job 19:19) What comfort there is in fellowship, in being surrounded by those who love us and who have understood our plight in life!

God even restored Job's family to him. *"He had also seven sons and three daughters."* (Job 42:13) Isn't it interesting that even the number of Job's children was doubled because he still had the ten that had gone to heaven? They were alive in the heavenlies. And now he receives ten more children!

"So the Lord blessed the latter end of Job more than his beginning. So Job died, being old and full of days." (Job 42:12a, 17)

What a happy ending to a miserable situation. It seems too good to be true in some ways. Yet Paul writes of Him *"who is able to do exceedingly abundantly above all that we ask or think."* (Ephesians 3:20)

Are we expecting Him to bless our lives in the same way? He promises to do just that. (Romans 8:28) Are we able to see even that which is evil as from the hand of the Lord? (Job 42:11) This is the deep wisdom and changeless faith that God has worked into Job's life.

CHAPTER SEVEN

CONCLUDING CONSIDERATIONS

Some may be tempted to say, "Job was a unique case of God's dealings with men. We cannot generalize from the teachings in Job." And, of course, it is true that God's plan in each life is unique. However, the basic truths about the character of God are unchanging. And we learn much about the character and person of God in this Book.

The truths about God's sovereignty appear from Genesis to Revelation. And if we are going to have a right understanding about the Lord we must see this aspect of His Person.

David discovered God's hand active in every detail of his life: *"O Lord, thou hast searched me, and known me. Thou knowest my downsitting and mine uprising; thou understandest my thoughts afar off. Thou compassest my path and my lying down, and art acquainted with all my ways. For there is not a word in my tongue, but, lo, O Lord, thou knowest it altogether. Thou hast beset me behind and before, and laid thine hand upon me. Such knowledge is too wonderful for me; it is high, I cannot attain unto it."* (Psalm 139:1-6)

David was amazed at the intimate relationship that he had with the Father. He was assured of God's involvement in his sitting down, his standing up, his mundane thoughts, his going and his coming. God knew every word David would ever utter. And in verse six David is stating the truth that Job also discovered. He says that to understand this aspect of God's involvement in detail is beyond human comprehension. Only the Holy Spirit can reveal this Truth to us.

David continues his description of the Lord: *"Whither shall I go from thy Spirit? Or whither shall I flee from thy presence? If I ascend up into heaven, thou art there; if I make my bed in hell, behold, thou art there. If I take the wings of the morning, and dwell in the uttermost parts of the sea, Even there shall thy hand lead me, and thy right hand shall hold me, If I say, Surely the darkness shall cover me; even the night shall be light about me. Yea, the darkness hideth not from thee, but the night shineth as the day; the darkness and the light are both alike to thee."* (Psalm 139:7-12)

David had discovered that God was at work in his life through the Person of the Holy Spirit continually. Even in those places of darkness where humanly we might think God would withdraw His hand, still He is with us. *"Being confident of this very thing that He who has begun the good work in you will continue to perform it until the day of Jesus Christ."* (Philippians 1:6)

God does not stop His work in us when we go off upon the paths of darkness. What a merciful God who took David's sin with Bathsheba and turned it to good, as it was through this union that the Messiah was born, this plan having been ordained before the foundation of the world.

David knew that his very personality and character, his weaknesses and his strengths, were aspects of his creation at the hand of God. *"For thou has possessed my inward parts; thou hast covered me in my mother's womb. I will praise thee; for I am fearfully and wonderfully made. Marvelous are thy works, and that my soul knoweth right well. My substance was not hidden from thee, when I was made in secret, and intricately wrought in the lowest parts of the earth. Thine eyes did see my substance, yet being unformed; and in thy book all my members were written, which in continuance were fashioned, when as yet there was none of them."* (Psalm 139:13-16)

David pictures God as having listed the very ingredients of his entire person in a book before he was yet created. God then followed His own planned formula in the creation of David as a person. What a majestic concept of God, as Creator and Father, comes as we see His total power. This is that "oldest lesson in the world" which provides the peace that exceeds our understanding. It is the lesson which Bullinger said, "is essential to our having peace with God." 6

This great understanding of God is the cornerstone of deep faith and eternal joy, experienced on a daily basis.

But many men and women in today's world, even Christian men and women, are in rebellion against the concept of God as sovereign over all. God has been depicted according to a very humanistic philosophy. We have been taught that God has chosen to limit Himself and depends upon humans to accomplish His work. We have heard God portrayed as lonesome and needy. We are sometimes told that He created men and women because He needed a love relationship.

Would God be God, complete and perfect, if He were needy, lacking in some area? Instead the Scripture says that He has "*predestinated us unto the adoption of sons by Jesus Christ to himself according to the good pleasure of his will, to the praise of the glory of His grace.*" (Ephesians 1:5, 6a) He created us simply for His own pleasure and glory.

God's Great Revelation to Us

As believers, as children of God by faith in Jesus Christ, we desire to live a stable life, rooted and grounded in Christ. We sense identification with Paul as he declared the desire of his life.

"That I may know him, and the power of his resurrection, and the fellowship of his sufferings, being made conformable unto his death." (Philippians 3:10)

The great news of the gospel is that our Shepherd is faithfully caring for us, His sheep. *"Now the God of peace, that brought again from the dead our Lord Jesus, that great Shepherd of the sheep, through the blood of the everlasting covenant, Make you perfect in every good work to do his will, working in you that which is well-pleasing in his sight, through Jesus Christ, to whom be glory forever and ever. Amen."* (Hebrews 13:20, 21)

We can be assured that He loves us as fully as He loves His Son Jesus Christ. He will remain faithful to us, even when we are faithless. And, even the suffering of this present time is an integral part of His highest and best for us. And He _will_ bring us from darkness to light.

"Now unto him that is able to keep you from falling, and to present you faultless before the presence of his glory with exceeding joy, to the only wise God, our Savior, be glory and majesty, dominion and power, both now and ever. Amen." (Jude 24, 25)

CHAPTER EIGHT

CLOSING THOUGHTS

So, as we review the life of Job, what are the secrets God is revealing to us as believers about our own troubles and trials? We have had the privilege of seeing into the courts of heaven where God and Satan confer; we have listened in on a personal conversation between God and Job and their relationship; we have seen the "end of Job" which was better than his beginning full of God's double blessings. What have we learned?

Here are some of the great truths that the Lord wants us to know and walk in, amidst every trial, tragedy or inconvenience:

1. God alone determines our circumstances – minute by minute. (Ephesians 1:11; Proverbs 16:9)

2. His complete and total purpose is to conform us to the image of Christ. (Romans 8:28-29)

3. He alone knows what we need to bring us to new levels of trust and faith. Jesus Christ, who was sinless, laid down His life willingly in order to accomplish the Father's purpose. God is bringing us to that same level of willingness. (Matthew 16:25)

4. Let us remember the words of Paul when he had his battle with Satan: *"For this thing I besought the Lord thrice, that it might depart from me. And he said unto me,*

*My grace is sufficient for thee; for my strength is made perfect in weakness. Most gladly, therefore, will I rather glory in my infirmities, that the power of Christ may rest upon me. Therefore, I take pleasure in infirmities (*weaknesses*), in persecutions, in distresses, for Christ's sake; for when I am weak, then am I strong.*" (2 Corinthians 12:8-10)

The Lord is always walking us into weakness. He desires for us to embrace it joyfully, to glory in our weakness, to take pleasure in our trials! That is the privilege we have! To give up, praise Him and watch and wait!

James writes, *"My brethren, count it all joy when ye fall into various trials."* (James 1:2) The Lord is always showing us our inadequacy and His complete adequacy. May we embrace every trial, temptation, struggle, frustration, irritation, inconvenience, hurt, and depression enthusiastically! For His strength will be demonstrated in these difficult places.

5. Most of our friends (and some relatives) will not believe that our misfortunes and failures are God's hand at work. Thus we will feel guilty, condemned, and discouraged if we take our eyes off our sovereign God.

6. God is love. His banner over us is love. All things are flowing from His heart of love to each of us as believers.

7. May we dare to tell Him exactly how we feel in our circumstances. He promises to reveal Himself in response to our honesty.

8. May we throw ourselves upon His grace and mercy. He is merciful and He will bless us because he loves us.

Bullinger, E.W., *The Book of Job*, Kregel Publications, Grand Rapids, Michigan, 1990.
*   Footnotes 1, 2 p. viii; 3, p. ix; 6, p. 92

Reichert, Rabbi Dr. Victor E., *Job,* The Soncino Press, Hindhead, Surrey, 1946, page 219
*   Footnote 5, p.84

Scofield, C.I. DD, The New Scofield Reference Bible, King James Version, Oxford University Press, New York, 1967

Thielicke, Helmut, *The Silence of God,* William B. Eerdmans Publishing Company, Grand Rapids, Michigan, 1962.
*   Footnote 4, p.78

Glenna Salsbury, a graduate of Northwestern University, holds a Masters Degree from UCLA and a Masters of Theology from Fuller Seminary.

Throughout her adult life, she has been actively involved in Christian ministry. She's hosted her own national cable television show, "Let's Study the Bible" for more than five years and a radio talk show, "A Visit With Glenna." Along with writing a column, which targeted the teenage audience for Scripture Press International, she has served as a full-time staff member of Young Life, a teaching leader and representative for Bible Study Fellowship.

Currently Glenna provides Christian leadership and development programs, Bible Study retreats, and Christian conference programming, nationally and internationally.
After forming her own company, Salsbury Enterprises, in 1980 she has expanded into customer service training and being a keynote speaker for many of the Fortune 500 companies.

An active member of the National Speakers Association (NSA), Glenna earned the coveted CSP (Certified Speaking Professional) designation given by NSA. In 1990 she received the CPAE Speaker Hall of Fame Award (Council of Peers Award for Excellence) - one of only a handful of women in the world to hold this honor. Glenna was the 1997-98 President of NSA.

Glenna was married to the late Jim Salsbury, former Detroit Lion and Green Bay Packer. She spends much of her free time with her three daughters and 5 grandchildren.

ADDITIONAL INFORMATION

For additional information write to the address given below. Other materials are available. These include books, cassette tapes and study materials. Glenna is also available for presentations at retreats, conferences and seminars.

Glenna Salsbury
9228 N. 64th Place
Paradise Valley, Arizona 85253 USA
Phone: 480 483-7732
Fax: 480 483-2615

Email: ISpeak4U@aol.com
http://www.GlennaSalsbury.com